TECH BYTES
EXPLORING SPACE

VISITING SPACE

BY JOYCE MARKOVICS

NORWOOD HOUSE PRESS

NORWOOD HOUSE PRESS

Cover: A NASA astronaut in space.

For more information about Norwood House Press, please visit our website at: www.norwoodhousepress.com or call 866-565-2900.

Book Designer: Ed Morgan
Editorial and Production: Bowerbird Books
Content Consultant: Dr. Joel Green, Astrophysicist

Photo Credits: NASA, cover and title page; NASA, 4–5; NASA, 5; NASA, ESA, CSA, and STScI, 6; NASA Goddard/Bill Hrybyk, 7; NASA, 8; NASA, 9; Wikimedia Commons, 10; Wikimedia Commons, 11; Wikimedia Commons/Sailko, 12; Public Domain, 13; Wikimedia Commons, 14; Public Domain, 15; Wikimedia Commons/AElfwine, 16; NASA, 17; Wikimedia Commons/Gregory R Todd, 18; NASA/JPL-Caltech, 19; NASA/JPL, 20; Library of Congress/ Leffler, Warren K, photographer, 21; Wikimedia Commons/Tempe, 22; Wikimedia Commons/Arto Jousi/Suomen valokuvataiteen museo/Alma Media/Uuden Suomen kokoelma; Restored by Adam Cuerden, 23; NASA, 24; Wikimedia Commons/Alexander Mokletsov, 25 top; NASA, 25 bottom; NASA, 26; NASA/Neil Armstrong, 27; NASA/Jet Propulsion Laboratory, 29; NASA, 30; NASA/CXC/NGST, 31; NASA, 32; NASA, 33; NASA/JPL-Caltech, 19 right; NASA, 19 left; ESA & MPS for OSIRIS Team MPS/UPD/LAM/IAA/RSSD/INTA/UPM/DASP/IDA, 35; © Dotted Yetu/ Shutterstock,36–37; NASA, 38; Wikimedia Commons/Skyway, 39; Wikimedia Commons/Kevin M. Gill, 39; Wikimedia Commons/Skatebiker, 41 top; ESO/DSS, 41 bottom; NASA, ESA, CSA, STScI, 42–43.

Hardcover ISBN: 978-1-68450-726-9
Paperback ISBN: 978-1-68404-840-3

Library of Congress Cataloging-in-Publication Data has been filed and is available at catalog.loc.gov

359N—012023
Manufactured in the United States of America in North Mankato, Minnesota.

CONTENTS

Words that are bolded in the text are defined in the glossary.

CHAPTER 1
SEEING SPACE

On July 12, 2022, the James Webb Space Telescope released images of the universe that shocked the world. As tall as a three-story building and as long as a tennis court, the telescope is the largest and most powerful space observatory ever built. The Webb's pictures showed ancient galaxies that sparkled like colorful jewels. They also revealed new stars emerging from enormous clouds of interstellar dust. In addition to capturing images of the first galaxies ever formed, the Webb telescope has the ability to observe planets and other objects in our solar system. It can see where new planets and stars are forming. This cutting-edge telescope will also gather information about the atmospheres of planets orbiting other stars in our universe. These planets, known as exoplanets, could hold signs of life.

This image—called the Cosmic Cliffs—captured by the James Webb telescope shows new stars being born.

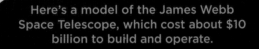

Here's a model of the James Webb Space Telescope, which cost about $10 billion to build and operate.

DID YOU KNOW?

The James Webb Space Telescope is orbiting the Sun about 1 million miles (1.5 million km) from Earth! Its huge mirrors are coated with a very thin layer of gold.

When the Webb telescope peers out into space, it's like looking back in time! Light travels quickly—at 186,000 miles per second (300,000 km/sec). However, space is incredibly vast. It's so gigantic that the time it takes light to travel in space is noticeable to scientists. In space, travel is measured in light-years. A light-year is the distance light travels in one Earth year. This distance is about 6 trillion miles (9.5 trillion km). For example, when scientists observe a star that's ten light-years away, they see it as it existed ten years ago when light first left the star's surface. So, the farther away a star or galaxy, the older the light coming from it is.

Of the many images taken by the James Webb telescope, some show galaxies that were created 11, 12, and 13 billion years ago! That's not long after our entire universe formed. The Webb's first images were presented during a ceremony at the Goddard Space Flight Center. As the pictures appeared on a big screen, people *oohed* and *aahed*. They couldn't contain their excitement. "I'm gobsmacked," said one astronomer.

This is another Webb telescope image of deep space. Each speck is a galaxy. The universe is thought to contain 200 billion galaxies!

THE GODDARD SPACE FLIGHT CENTER

The Goddard Space Flight Center is a NASA research laboratory in Greenbelt, Maryland. It's NASA's first and oldest space center and employs around 10,000 people. The facility was named after Robert H. Goddard, an American rocket scientist, born in 1882. Goddard built the world's first liquid-fueled rocket, which led to the development of spacecraft in the 1950s.

The Goddard Space Flight Center in Maryland

The James Webb Space Telescope before it was launched into space

The scientists who saw the Webb telescope's images were floored not only by the beauty of the images but by the information they contained about our universe. "That was always out there," said astrophysicist Jane Rigby, who works on the Webb. "We just had to build a telescope to go see what was there." Since the Webb telescope was launched on December 25, 2021, Rigby and her team at NASA have been working around the clock. Their goal is to discover as much as they can about the first galaxies in the universe, exoplanets, and more. John Mather, another Webb scientist said, "We're looking for the first things to come out of the Big Bang."

ASTROPHYSICIST
JANE RIGBY

Jane Rigby studies how galaxies evolve and grow over time using various telescopes, including the Webb. She loves talking with the public about science and being a queer role model. "Inclusion matters," said Rigby. When asked about the James Webb Space Telescope, she said, "I'm so proud of helping that telescope become a reality." Rigby continued, "Give me a telescope and I can come up with something good to do with it."

Jane Rigby taking a selfie in front of the Magellan Clay Telescope in Atacama, Chile

The BIG BANG

About 13.8 billion years ago, the entire universe was as tiny as a dot made by a pencil tip, and it was extremely hot. The heat caused this super-small point to expand in an event called the Big Bang. When this happened, the universe expanded very rapidly, growing many times larger in a fraction of a second. At that time, the universe was like a hot soup containing different tiny particles. Then the universe expanded some more and cooled. There was darkness for a few hundred million years. After that, the particles grouped to form the first stars and eventually the first galaxies. More and more stars and light formed and galaxies crashed together, leading to planets, comets, and other objects in space. People hope to find out what the universe's first light and stars looked like with the James Webb Space Telescope. It's one of many technological tools scientists use to explore space.

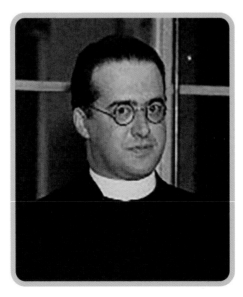

Georges Lemaître was a Catholic priest who's credited with coming up with the Big Bang theory.

DID YOU KNOW?

In 1927, astronomer Georges Lemaître claime that the universe started as a small, single point. He also said that the universe stretched and expanded to become what it is today and that it could keep on growing

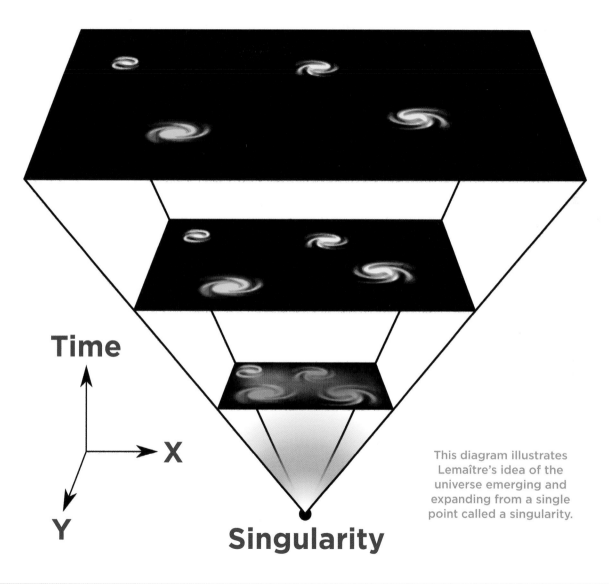

Time

X

Y

Singularity

This diagram illustrates Lemaître's idea of the universe emerging and expanding from a single point called a singularity.

CHAPTER 2
SPACE EXPLORATION

Throughout history, people have been captivated by the idea of visiting space. Since humans first looked up at the sky, they have wondered about the universe and how it worked. In 1609, an Italian astronomer named Galileo used a simple telescope to observe the sky. Although what Galileo saw through the telescope was small and fuzzy, he could still see hills, valleys, and craters on the Moon! He also saw an area of light that curved across the sky. This would later be identified as the Milky Way Galaxy—our home in the universe.

As time passed, telescopes became more advanced. Astronomers discovered new stars and how to calculate the distances between them. However, telescopes used on the ground are not a perfect tool. Why? Earth's atmosphere distorts the light coming from stars. So when scientists use telescopes to view stars, they also see the distortion. It's similar to looking at an object through a glass of water.

Galileo was born in 1564 and died in 1642. He is known as the father of astronomy and modern science.

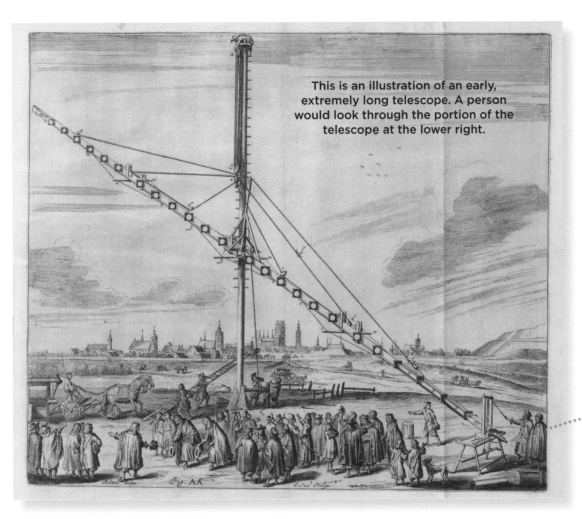

This is an illustration of an early, extremely long telescope. A person would look through the portion of the telescope at the lower right.

In the 1800s, scientists invented new technology known as a spectroscope that can separate light by its wavelengths. This tool helped astronomers understand more about the composition and movement of planets and other objects in space. Scientists thought more and more about visiting space one day.

REACHING SPACE

Over time, scientists gained more and more knowledge about the workings of the solar system. During the twentieth century, visiting space become less of a dream and more of an achievable goal. A Russian scientist named Konstantin Tsiolkovsky (1857–1935) was one of the first scientists to begin to figure out how humans could actually travel to space. How would they get there? *Rockets*, thought Tsiolkovsky! He wrote about using rockets to launch orbital spaceships. He also thought up ways to launch and fly the rockets, as well as the ideal shape and fuel for them. Tsiolkovsky said, "Earth is the cradle of humanity, but mankind cannot stay in the cradle forever."

Konstantin Tsiolkovsky spent most of his life living in a log house not far from Moscow. Here he is with some of his models for space vehicles.

THE **EARLIEST** **SCIENCE** **FICTION**

Throughout the centuries, scientific discoveries about space have inspired writers. Galileo's work with telescopes prompted authors to create science fiction stories about space exploration. One of the earliest science-fiction writers was Cyrano de Bergerac. In his 1649 book *The Voyage to the Moon*, he describes the main character trying to reach the Moon. In one attempt, he jumps into a "spacecraft" powered by firecrackers. This was the first ever description of a rocket-powered space flight!

Cyrano de Bergerac was a French writer who lived from 1619 to 1655. This is an engraving of his self-named character, Cyrano, trying to reach the Moon.

Thanks to Konstantin Tsiolkovsky and other great scientists' contributions, space travel was becoming more feasible. Then World War II (1939–1945) happened, and the field of rocket science took off. By the 1940s, most of the countries that were involved in the war came up with their own rocket technology. Some countries invented rocket-powered aircraft. Germany was the leader in the field because of a scientist named Werner von Braun. He and his team invented one of the most important rockets ever made, the V-2. Von Braun's 46-foot (14-m) tall rocket had a novel engine design that allowed the machine to fly high and fast. Sadly, at the time, the rocket was used for war and not space travel. However, the rocket directly led to the creation of others that would eventually carry spacecraft and humans to space.

A replica of the V-2 rocket on display

After World War II came a time known as the Cold War. It was a long, tense period between the United States and the Soviet Union. With hostility growing between the countries, both worked on new, powerful rockets that could carry weapons across continents. Then the Soviets developed a rocket called the R7, which signaled the start of what was referred to as the "space race."

Scientist Werner von Braun stands next to a rocket.

DID YOU KNOW?

Werner von Braun (1912–1977) was fascinated by science fiction and space exploration as a child. From his teenage years on, he never stopped being curious and learning about space travel. He fled Nazi Germany in 1944 to work and live in the United States for the rest of his life.

The
SPACE
RACE

On October 4, 1957, the Soviet Union used the R7 rocket to launch a beach ball-sized satellite called Sputnik 1 into space. It was a monumental achievement. Sputnik 1 marked the first ever human-made object placed in orbit around Earth! Sputnik 1 was a shiny metal sphere that contained a thermometer, batteries, radio, and had four pointy radio antennas sticking out of it. After arriving in space, Sputnik 1 used its onboard radio transmitter to send out signals in the form of beeps to a crew on Earth. The satellite orbited Earth once every 98 minutes. After Sputnik 1, the Soviets launched another larger satellite. They named it Sputnik 2, and it carried a living creature—a dog named Laika!

Sputnik 1, the world's first orbital satellite

DID YOU KNOW?

Sputnik 1 means "fellow traveler" in Russian. The satellite fell back to Earth in 1958, less than a year after it was launched.

The launch of Sputnik shocked the United States. Worried that Russia might also be developing weapons that could be operated from space, America took action. In response to Sputnik, the United States launched its own satellites. On January 31, 1958, the U.S. satellite Explorer 1 successfully orbited Earth, thanks in large part to Werner von Braun's rocket technology. That same year, the U.S. government created NASA to further explore space as well as to compete with the Soviets in the space race.

Explorer 1 being launched by the United States

NASA

NASA further developed the United States's space program. It quickly began managing the Jet Propulsion Laboratory (JPL), a space research development center, in California. One of NASA's primary goals was to put a human in space. This prompted NASA's Project Mercury, which lasted from 1959 to 1963. The project included six spaceflights to put astronauts in space. NASA selected seven young, fit jet pilots to become astronauts. They were called the Mercury Seven. At the same time, the Soviets were also preparing their own people—called cosmonauts—for space exploration. Yuri Gagarin was one of the cosmonauts. As both countries worked around the clock to send a person to space, one country edged ahead.

NASA's logo on a Jet Propulsion Laboratory (JPL) building in Pasadena, California

THE NATIONAL DEFENSE EDUCATION ACT

As a reaction to the space race, the U.S. Congress passed the National Defense Education Act (NDEA) to improve science and math education. According to the law, it would "ensure trained manpower of sufficient quality and quantity to meet the national defense needs of the United States." The U.S. government wanted to prepare its young people to defend their country from outside threats, such as the Soviet Union. The NDEA was the first nationwide education law ever passed.

The NDEA was signed into law in 1958. This photo shows students in a classroom that same year improving their science and math skills.

CHAPTER 3
HUMANS in SPACE

On April 12, 1961, Soviet cosmonaut Yuri Gagarin became the first human to reach space and orbit Earth. He rode in a Vostok 1 spacecraft that was propelled by an R7 rocket. The space flight lasted 108 minutes. Although the Vostok 1 had manual controls, the Soviets steered the craft from the ground. Why? They were uncertain how the human body would function in space. Fortunately, Gagarin had no physical issues. He re-entered the atmosphere in a descent capsule and safely parachuted to the ground. "Orbiting Earth in the spaceship, I saw how beautiful our planet is. People, let us preserve and increase this beauty, not destroy it!" Gagarin said about his journey.

About three weeks later, NASA sent astronaut Alan Shepard to space. He went on a short fifteen-minute flight but never fully orbited Earth. Proud of the accomplishment but wanting more, President John F. Kennedy declared: "I believe that this nation should commit itself to achieving the goal, before the decade is out, of landing a man on the Moon." Did the United States have a chance of meeting this target?

The instrument panel in the Vostok 1 spacecraft

VOSTOK 1 FLIGHT ISSUES

Yuri Gagarin became famous around the world after being the first person to travel to space.

Though it was a success overall, the Vostok 1 space flight was not problem-free. When the capsule reentered Earth's atmosphere, it started to spin wildly. "As soon as the braking rocket shut off, there was a sharp jolt, and the craft began to rotate around its axis at a very high velocity," said Gagarin. The spinning was caused by a piece of equipment that initially failed to disconnect from the descent capsule. Thankfully, the problem lasted for only a few minutes.

In 1962, the United States succeeded in sending a human into orbit. Even though astronaut John Glenn's trip only lasted five hours, it excited Americans. During the 1960s, NASA took important steps to put a person on the Moon. Project Gemini helped astronauts learn how to steer and dock a spacecraft. It also helped them practice going on a spacewalk.

Gemini 6A (top) and 7 (bottom) in December 1965

In addition, Project Gemini collected information about how spaceflight would affect astronauts' mental health. Being in a confined space with a small group of people can impact an astronaut's state of mind. NASA learned how to prepare astronauts for life in space. After Gemini came the Apollo missions, which would change space exploration forever.

Edward White during a spacewalk for a Gemini mission in 1965

Before becoming a cosmonaut, Valentina Tereshkova worked in a factory.

DID YOU KNOW?

In 1963, the Soviets sent the first woman to space! Her name is Valentina Tereshkova. She spent three days in space, orbited Earth 48 times, and is the only woman in history to travel solo to space.

APOLLO MISSIONS

There were many Apollo missions. They were designed to land humans on the Moon and safely bring them back to Earth. Not all went smoothly. In fact, some ended in disaster. However, each mission returned a wealth of scientific information. In July 1969, Apollo 11 launched from Kennedy Space Center in Merritt Island, Florida, with three astronauts bound for the Moon! They were Neil Armstrong, Buzz Aldrin, and Michael Collins.

Apollo 11 liftoff from Kennedy Space Center

After a rough landing on the Moon's jagged surface, the astronauts were scheduled to nap, but they were too excited to sleep. Not long after, Neil Armstrong put on his bulky spacesuit and stepped out onto the surface of the Moon. He famously said it was, "one small step for man—one giant leap for mankind." Buzz Aldrin followed him, becoming the second human on the Moon. They planted a flag and collected samples of lunar rocks and dust that would later be analyzed by scientists back on Earth. The Moon landing caused worldwide celebrations. It was the dawn of a new era of space exploration.

Buzz Aldrin walking on the Moon in 1969

DID YOU KNOW?

Gravity is the force on Earth that holds people on the ground. However, in space, astronauts and other things appear to float. There is a small amount of gravity—called microgravity—in space. Because microgravity is not very strong, it makes things seem weightless, including astronauts.

CHAPTER 4
OTHER TRIPS to SPACE

Other Moon landings followed. However, the United States wanted to travel beyond the Moon to explore the solar system. NASA did this with a series of unmanned satellites designed by the Jet Propulsion Laboratory and other partners. The Mariner program sent spacecraft to Venus, Mars, and Mercury for the first time in history. Images of the surfaces of Venus and Mars taken by the satellites helped NASA plan future trips. Other interplanetary missions followed. In the 1970s, Project Viking expanded on the Mariner program to investigate whether life could exist on Mars. Twin spacecraft, Viking 1 and 2, traveled to Mars to study and photograph the planet. The satellites monitored the weather to find out whether it could be hospitable to life. Viking 2 tested the Martian soil—called regolith—and discovered unusual chemicals in it. It was not clear to scientists whether these chemicals had come from living things. Yet the discovery prompted further studies and trips to Mars.

Mariner 2 was launched in 1962 and was the first interplanetary spacecraft.

SPACE SHUTTLES

Around the same time, NASA was developing a rocket-powered Space Shuttle that could make multiple trips to space. Columbia was the first Space Shuttle to reach orbit on April 12, 1981. Over the next two decades, Columbia carried dozens of astronauts to space. It spent more than 300 days in space and flew 28 missions. One of those missions involved transporting the Chandra X-ray Observatory to space. There were other Space Shuttle missions as well—135 in all—starting with Columbia and continuing with Challenger, Discovery, Atlantis, and Endeavor. Even after the tragic destruction of the Challenger shuttle in 1987, NASA launched many successful missions. The shuttles transported people to space, launched and repaired satellites, including the Hubble Space Telescope, and helped build the largest structure in space—the International Space Station (ISS). On its final mission in 2003, the Columbia broke apart during its reentry into Earth's atmosphere. All seven crewmembers died. NASA put new safety procedures in place to ensure that this kind of tragedy would never happen again. However, the disaster signaled the end of the Space Shuttle program. NASA's attention turned to a new space launch system and the International Space Station.

The Colombia Space Shuttle taking off

THE
CHANDRA
X-RAY
OBSERVATORY

The Chandra X-ray Observatory is a space telescope that picks up X-rays from very hot parts of the universe, such as exploded stars and matter around black holes. It was launched into space by the Space Shuttle Columbia in 1999. The Chandra X-ray Observatory is named after Subrahmanyan Chandrasekhar, a famous Indian astrophysicist.

The Chandra X-ray Observatory

SPACE STATION

The International Space Station, or ISS, is a huge spacecraft that orbits Earth about every 90 minutes. Many countries worked together to build the space station. The first section was launched in 1998, and other sections were added in the following years. In 2000, the first group of astronauts arrived to live on the ISS. Since that time, the space station has been home to groups of astronauts from different countries. The astronauts aboard the ISS conduct research about living and working in space. They study the effects of microgravity on the human body, test new technology, and perform many other experiments. The purpose of these experiments is to learn about living in space so humans can hopefully travel deeper into space one day.

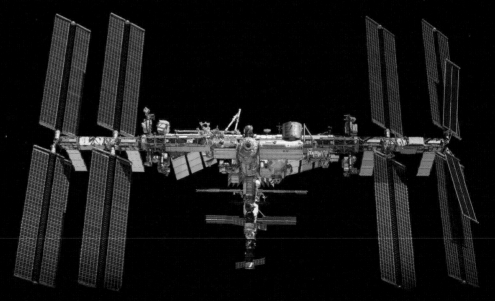

The ISS is about as big as a five-bedroom house and has two bathrooms. It travels at 17,000 miles (27,358 km) per hour!

THE STEADY SOYUZ

The Soyuz was first flown in 1967—and is one of the most reliable spacecraft ever invented. The Soyuz has been used to transport astronauts and supplies to and from the International Space Station. It's made up of three modules. The first section allows it to dock on the ISS. The middle part can carry up to three astronauts. The lower module holds equipment, such as communications devices. The Soyuz has made more than 140 flights to the ISS!

The Soyuz spacecraft

ROVERS

Technology has allowed people to live on the International Space Station. It has also made it possible for satellites to zoom past and orbit almost every planet in our solar system. In addition, humans have landed vehicles on some planets! In 2021, a car-sized NASA rover, called Perseverance, or Percy for short, landed on Mars. The robotic vehicle is searching for signs of life on the planet. It has high-tech cameras, radar that can pierce through solid ground, and lasers that can identify the chemical makeup of Martian rocks. One of Perseverance's most exciting tools is a small helicopter named Ingenuity. Ingenuity provides scientists with a bird's-eye view of Mars's surface. Experts are hoping it may pave the way for humans to visit Mars in the future, where the helicopter could be utilized to carry supplies. Percy will also be used to conduct experiments to find out, for example, how to make oxygen from the harsh Martian atmosphere. The rover will also collect rock samples that might contain signs of life!

The NASA rover Perseverance

Ingenuity, nicknamed Ginny, is the first aircraft to fly on another planet!

Mars is often called the Red Planet because of its color.

TOURING SPACE

In recent years, scientists and private companies have been researching and coming up with less expensive and faster ways to reach space—not just for astronauts but for space tourists! In 2001, an American businessman became the world's first space tourist to travel to space. Since then, space tourism has exploded, with multiple private companies offering trips to outer space. These companies include Space Adventures, Blue Origin, Axiom Space, Virgin Galactic, and SpaceX. The trips cost anywhere from hundreds of thousands to millions of dollars. So far, only a handful have taken place. In 2021, four individuals traveled on SpaceX's Crew Dragon spacecraft while it orbited Earth for three days.

Another company is offering trips to space in a pressurized cabin attached to a giant helium-filled balloon! "We go to space at 12 miles an hour, which means that it's very smooth and gentle. You're not rocketing away from Earth," said Jane Poynter, a founder of Space Perspective, a space balloon ride company. That's not all. Some companies are planning to build space hotels where people can stay after they reach space. One company's idea involves two ring-shaped properties that will orbit Earth and have luxury accommodations, including simulated gravity.

This is an artist's vision of a hotel in space.

With the help of private companies, NASA has plans to send astronauts, including the first woman and person of color, to the Moon—and beyond! NASA aims to have humans revisit the Moon and create a more permanent base camp there. With its partners, NASA is constructing the biggest rocket ever, the Space Launch System (SLS). The SLS will be as tall as a skyscraper and powerful enough to carry more than 100 tons (91 m tons) to space. It will be responsible for propelling the Orion spacecraft and Gateway lunar command module, where astronauts can live and work, to the Moon. Once on the Moon, NASA is aiming to install a lunar cabin and mobile home there! There will also be a rover for exploring the crater-filled surface of the Moon. What scientists learn about the Moon during these missions will prepare them to go deeper in space—and, perhaps, to Mars!

Pictured is what a base camp on the Moon could look like.

SPACE ELEVATOR

In the 1890s, Konstantin Tsiolkovsky came up with the idea for a space elevator when he first saw the Eiffel Tower in Paris, France. He dreamed of an elevator that stretched from Earth to space. The space elevator idea gained followers over the years. Why? It would permit space vehicles and astronauts to visit space at a low cost and without the use of rockets. However, building such an elevator is no easy task. It would require a long cable and anchor in space that would spin around Earth to keep the cable taut— much like the ball in a game of tetherball.

This is a diagram for a space elevator.

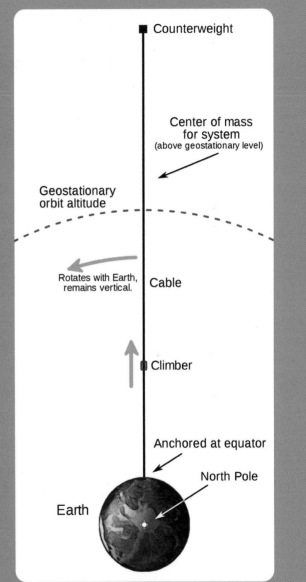

Counterweight

Center of mass
for system
(above geostationary level)

Geostationary
orbit altitude

Rotates with Earth,
remains vertical.

Cable

Climber

Anchored at equator

North Pole

Earth

In addition to visiting the Moon and Mars, scientists are also investigating traveling to other stars. Breakthrough Starshot is one such project. It aims to send tiny robotic probes that are equipped with sails to Alpha Centauri. This star system is about 4.37 light-years away and contains at least one exoplanet—Proxima Cen b—that could possibly support life. The goal is to launch a "mothership" that would carry and release about a thousand small spacecraft. Each one is about the size of a postage stamp. A laser on Earth would focus a beam of light on the probes' sails to accelerate them to superfast speeds. The probes would then zoom through space at 20 percent the speed of light! If all goes accordingly, Starshot craft could reach Alpha Centauri in a little over 20 years. Once at their destination, the probes would take many photos. The scientists working on the project have a 30-year plan to get the project off the ground.

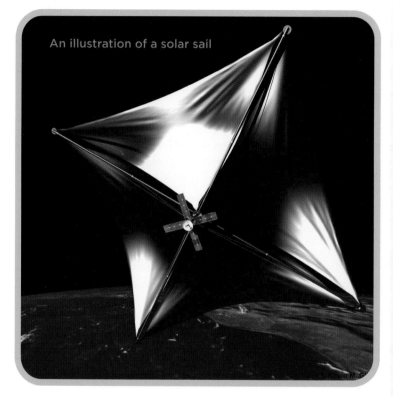

An illustration of a solar sail

The bright star on the left is Alpha Centauri.
The circled area is Proxima Centauri.

Alpha Centauri.

DID YOU KNOW?

Alpha Centauri is a yellow
star that's similar to our Sun,
although it's slightly larger.

In the meantime, there is still much more for current space technology to do to help humans explore space. For example, the James Webb Space Telescope will continue looking at distant worlds and stars to help us understand the history of our universe. Other satellites will be used to study planets in our solar system as well as Earth itself. Today, Earth is reacting to climate change and other issues, and satellites can help us track what's happening. The International Space Station, too, will be utilized until 2031 when NASA plans to retire the aging satellite and then work with companies to build a new one. As humans have since the beginning of time, they will keep looking to the stars and space and wondering what our place is in the universe. Are we alone? Science and technology will hopefully help us answer that question one day.

This James Webb image shows the remains of a star after it shed its outer layers.

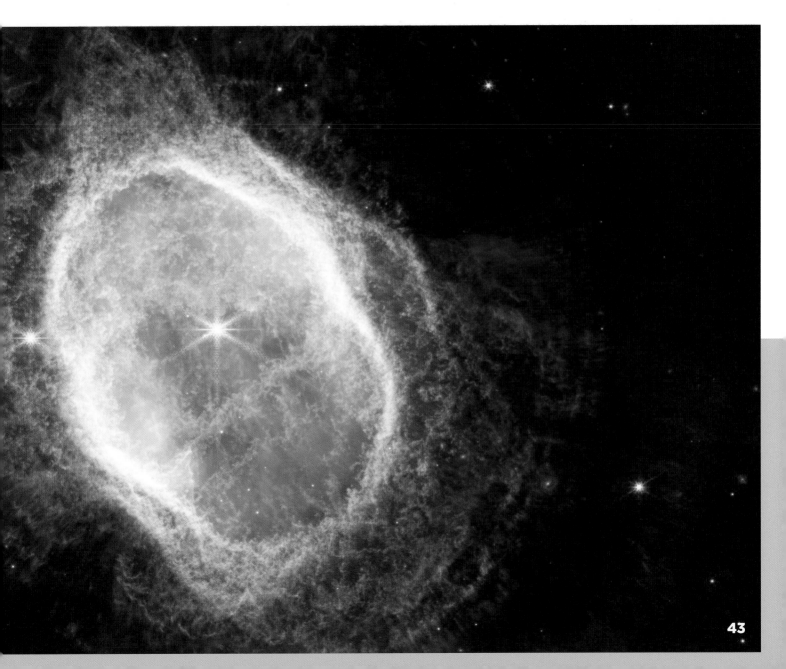

GLOSSARY

accelerate (ak-SEL-uh-rate): to speed up.

antennas (an-TEN-uhz): rods, wires, or other devices used to transmit or receive radio or TV signals.

astronauts (ASS-truh-nawts): people who travel into space.

astronomer (uh-STRON-uh-mur): a scientist who studies outer space.

astrophysicist (as-troh-FIZ-ih-sist): a scientist who studies the universe and stars and planets.

atmospheres (AT-muhss-fihrz): the mixtures of gases surrounding Earth and other planets.

axis (AK-sis): a straight central part in a structure to which other parts are connected.

black holes (BLAK HOHLZ): regions of space having a gravitational field so intense that no matter or light can escape.

captivated (KAP-tuh-veyt-uhd): held the attention of.

climate change (KLYE-mit CHAYNJ): the warming of Earth's air and oceans due to environmental changes, such as a buildup of greenhouse gases that trap the Sun's heat in Earth's atmosphere.

comets (KOM-itz): objects in space consisting of ice and dust.

composition (kom-puh-ZISH-uhn): the way in which a whole or mixture is made up.

continents (KON-tuhn-uhnts): any of the world's seven main continuous expanses of land.

descent (dih-SENT): the act of moving downward.

distorts (dih-STAWRTS): presents inaccurately.

feasible (FEE-zuh-buhl): capable of being done.

galaxies (GAL-uhk-seez): large groups of millions or billions of stars, gas, and dust held together by gravity.

gobsmacked (GOB-smaktd): astonished.

hospitable (HOS-pi-tuh-buhl): pleasant and favorable for living in.

hostility (ho-SYIL-ih-tee): unfriendliness.

humanity (hyoo-MAN-uh-tee): all people.

inclusion (in-KLOO-zhuhn): the state of being included.

interplanetary (in-ter-PLAN-ih-ter-ee): occurring between the planets or between a planet and the Sun.

interstellar dust (in-ter-STEL-er DUHST): dry, fine particles in space.

laboratory (LAB-ruh-tor-ee): a place used by scientists to conduct experiments.

manual (MAN-yoouhl): worked by hand; not by machine.

modules (MOJ-oolz): independent self-contained units of a spacecraft.

monumental (mon-yuh-MEN-tuhl): exceptionally great.

NASA (NAS-ah): the National Aeronautics and Space Administration; the government agency in charge of the U.S. space program.

novel (NOV-uhl): a book that tells a long made-up story.

observatory (uhb-ZUR-vuh-tor-ee): a place or building for viewing stars and planets.

orbiting (OR-bit-ing): moving around something in space in a circular, continuous path.

parachuted (PAH-ruh-shoot-uhd): jumped with a parachute from a plane, helicopter, or space capsule.

pressurized (PRESH-ur-rized): made to keep air in a sealed environment such as a space suit.

propelled (pruh-PELD): moved or pushed forward.

queer (KWEER): relating to a sexual or gender identity that does not correspond to established ideas of sexuality and gender, especially heterosexual norms.

radar (RAY-dar): a tool that can find the location of an object by sending out radio waves, which hit the object and bounce back to form an image on a computer screen.

satellite (SAT-uh-lite): a spacecraft sent into outer space to gather and send back information.

simulated (SIM-yuh-lay-tid): pretended to be like something real.

Soviet Union (SOH-vee-uht YOON-yuhn): a former country that was centered around Russia.

telescope (TEL-uh-skohp): a tool for making things that are far away appear bigger.

thermometer (thur-MOM-uh-tur): an instrument that shows the temperature of something, such as the air.

transmitter (transs-MIT-er): equipment that is used for sending signals or messages.

velocity (vuh-LOS-ih-tee): the rate of speed at which something happens.

FOR MORE INFORMATION

Books

Aguilar, David A. *Space Encyclopedia*. Washington, DC: National Geographic, 2020.
Tour the solar system and beyond in this comprehensive book on space exploration.

Anderson, Amy, and Brian Anderson. *Space Dictionary for Kids*. New York, NY: Routledge, 2016.
Learn all about rockets, astronauts, the universe, and the fascinating world of space exploration.

DeGrasse Tyson, Neil. *Astrophysics for Young People in a Hurry*. New York, NY: Norton Young Readers, 2019.
Read about the mysteries of the universe in this accessible and exciting book.

Koontz, Robin. *Our Place in Space*. Vero Beach, FL: Rourke Educational Media, 2016.
Explore Earth's place in the universe and learn space-related facts.

Websites

NASA Kids' Club (https://www.nasa.gov/kidsclub/index.html)
NASA provides an online place for children to play as they learn about NASA and its missions.

NASA Science Space Place (https://spaceplace.nasa.gov)
NASA's award-winning Space Place website engages children in space and Earth science through interactive games, hands-on activities, and more.

National Geographic Kids—Facts About Mars (https://www.natgeokids.com/uk/discover/science/space/facts-about-mars/)
Young readers will uncover cool facts about the Red Planet.

National Geographic Kids—History of Space Travel (https://kids.nationalgeographic.com/space/article/history-of-space-travel)
Learn about the history of humans traveling into space.

Space Center Houston (https://spacecenter.org/exhibits-and-experiences/journey-to-space/)
Space Center Houston is a leading science and space exploration learning center.

Places to Visit
Kennedy Space Center in Merritt Island, FL
(https://www.kennedyspacecenter.com/?utm_source=google&utm_medium=yext)
NASA's Kennedy Space Center features exhibits and historic spacecraft and memorabilia.

The National Air and Space Museum in Washington, DC
(https://www.si.edu/museums/air-and-space-museum)
The National Air and Space Museum maintains the world's largest and most significant collection of aviation and space artifacts.

Rose Center for Earth and Space in New York, NY
(https://www.amnh.org/exhibitions/permanent/rose-center)
Explore the cosmos, the history of the universe, galaxies, Earth, and more at the Rose Center at the American Museum for Natural History.

INDEX

ABOUT THE AUTHOR

Joyce Markovics has written hundreds of books for kids. She lives in an old house along the Hudson River. She is fascinated by space and all the things we still don't know about the universe. Joyce would like to dedicate this book to Kaia and Addie White, two curious explorers.